A LETTER TO PHILIP HOFER

HARVARD COLLEGE LIBRARY MS. TYP 410

JAN VAN KRIMPEN

A LETTER TO PHILIP HOFER ON CERTAIN PROBLEMS CONNECTED WITH THE MECHANICAL CUTTING OF PUNCHES

A FACSIMILE REPRODUCTION

WITH AN INTRODUCTION AND COMMENTARY BY

JOHN DREYFUS

DEPARTMENT OF PRINTING AND GRAPHIC ARTS

HARVARD COLLEGE LIBRARY

CAMBRIDGE / MASSACHUSETTS

DAVID R. GODINE / BOSTON

1972

STUDIES IN THE HISTORY OF CALLIGRAPHY AND PRINTING, 4

CONTENTS

PREFACE

The Department of Printing and Graphic Arts of Harvard University's Houghton Library was founded in 1941 by Philip Hofer, who served as Curator until his retirement in 1968. His many interests are reflected in publications bearing the imprint of this Department, and in 1947, in cooperation with the Newberry Library, Chicago, he began the series, *Studies in the History of Calligraphy*, a field in which he maintained a special interest. The first item in the series was *Luminario, or the Third Book of the Liber Elementorum by G.B. Verini*, in an English version by A.F. Johnson with an introduction by Stanley Morison. Second in the series, in 1954, was *The First Writing Book, an English Translation & Facsimile Text of Arrighi's Operina*, with an introduction and notes by John Howard Benson. The third item, in 1959, was *American Writing Masters and Copybooks, History and Bibliography through Colonial Times* by Ray Nash.

With the publication of Jan van Krimpen's *A Letter to Philip Hofer*, the series has now been expanded to *Studies in the History of Calligraphy and Printing*. This fourth volume attests to another of Philip Hofer's interests – lettering and typography – and to the special role he has played in forming the collections of the Department of Printing and Graphic Arts.

A Letter to Philip Hofer was a commissioned manuscript which evolved through an exchange of correspondence. Van Krimpen wrote Hofer from Haarlem in July 1953, the year of Enschedé's jubilee exhibition: 'I have been thinking over your request & I think that if I can find time I can do what you have asked me. The only interesting thing, in my opinion, is the problem I think I mentioned to you: a problem which I doubt I shall ever be able

9

to solve for myself. How can a living design, made by human hand, eye (& heart), be adequately rendered by the mechanical means now in use of producing type?' Two years and twelve letters later, and after a personal meeting in Florence, Van Krimpen wrote Hofer on November 1955, '...the manuscript is finished: Laus Deo.'

PETER A. WICK

INTRODUCTION AND COMMENTARY

'I am becoming something of an author', Van Krimpen wrote to me on 1 March 1956. He had written to me frequently since publication four years earlier of my book on *The Work of Jan van Krimpen*. But there was a special reason why he chose to tell me in March 1956 of the manuscript which he had completed five months earlier for Philip Hofer. At Van Krimpen's request, payment for his work was on the way to me in England, so that I could keep him regularly supplied by post with English cigarettes, books and periodicals.

Van Krimpen read a great deal, in English and French, as well as in his Dutch mother tongue. But in neither language had he the facility to express himself in clear, simple prose. He constantly interrupted himself with qualifying clauses. So when the Harvard College Library and Mr Godine first asked me to write an introduction to this essay, I made a typescript of Van Krimpen's words and attempted to make them more easily intelligible by improving the punctuation. I also experimented with italics for emphasis, or for words which he proceeded to define. For a time I considered printing this version of his letter, as well as the photographic facsimile made from the original manuscript. But in the end I decided that it would be more helpful to print a résumé of his arguments and observations, and this will be found on pp. 19–22.

Soon it became obvious to me that the reader would need a great deal more background material for a full appreciation of what Van Krimpen had written. It was necessary to relate the contents of the manuscript to the other pieces he had written in the last years of his life, for he was quite accurate when he observed that he was becoming something of an author.

Still more was needed. Van Krimpen had discussed his ideas with a great many people, some of whom were mentioned by name in his text. The person to whom he devoted the greatest amount of space was his friend Stanley Morison, and as will later be explained more fully, I was particularly well placed to learn Morison's views on some of the topics discussed. After several readings of the Hofer manuscript, I decided to include opinions expressed by Morison, Updike, Rogers and others whom Van Krimpen mentioned, as well as such contemporaries as Eric Gill, Victor Hammer, Sem Hartz, Giovanni Mardersteig and Hermann Zapf, all of whom had wrestled with the same problems which *haunted* Van Krimpen (I use his own verb).

But before I tackle the subject matter of the Hofer manuscript I must explain how I became a friend of Van Krimpen and how I later became professionally involved in his work.

Towards the end of the Second World War, I was asked by two of Van Krimpen's English friends if I could obtain news of him, as they knew I was then with the army somewhere in Holland. These friends were Walter Lewis and Stanley Morison, with whom I had worked in Cambridge for a few months before I joined up. Lewis was University Printer; Morison was typographical adviser both to the Press and to the Monotype Corporation. Soon after their request reached me, I was in Haarlem and decided to drive to the ancient printing house of Enschedé en Zonen where Van Krimpen was employed. On the day I called he was working at home, so Mr Frans Enschedé piloted me out there and introduced me. Van Krimpen was delighted to have news from England, and invited me to come back again to see

Jan van Krimpen, sketch for an engraving by S. L. Hartz

P. H. Rädisch at work

him. I was able to spend two short leaves at his house before demobilization, and my return to Cambridge.

A few years later a publisher in Utrecht asked me to write a record of Van Krimpen's work in honour of his sixtieth birthday, and my book duly appeared in 1952. In that book I tried to give a full account of his work as designer of eighteen types, of numerous books, and also of many fine postage stamps, book labels and other items in which lettering played a prominent part. I was surprised that he had virtually taught himself the necessary skills, although he relied heavily upon the collaboration of an experienced punchcutter to translate his finished drawings into type. While I wrote the record, and while Van Krimpen supervised its printing, we kept up a lively correspondence. We also met at frequent intervals, for he had many friends and business contacts in London, and loved to visit them.

Before I left the army, I had brought back to Morison smoke proofs of punches for a new type which Van Krimpen had designed during the war. The Monotype Corporation agreed to cut this type, Spectrum by name, for mechanical composition, and thus renewed their pre-war association with this Dutch designer, whose Lutetia and Romulus types they had cut in the late twenties and early thirties.

In 1955 I was appointed typographical adviser to the Monotype Corporation, after several contacts with them over the making of a specially designed bible type for Cambridge. The cutting of the Spectrum series was not yet complete, and I learnt that Van Krimpen was a hard man to satisfy. On the shelves in Morison's office was a thick box file, with a spine label SPECTRUM TRIALS: the second word had a double significance – tribulations, and specimens. I had to take my share of the first, and examine in detail the second.

It was congenial work, for my admiration for Van Krimpen went back much further than ten years. I had first come across a specimen of his Lutetia type when reading *The Fleuron* at a time when I was supposed to be reading for a degree in economics at Cambridge. In *The Fleuron* no. V (1926) Morison had praised Lutetia as being 'a new type, underived from any historic predecessor or school' and 'exceedingly handsome'. I shared Morison's excitement over this design, and I also read with interest an essay by Van Krimpen on 'Typography in Holland' in *The Fleuron* no. VII (1930). I noticed later that the quality of the prose in that article bore the stamp of Morison's editorial hand. To my regret, Van Krimpen in his later years raised pained objections to any proposals to alter his English prose, except by Professor Ray Nash, who managed to improve those of Van Krimpen's essays which were published in *Printing and Graphic Arts*.

Van Krimpen had a very high regard for Morison and Nash, both of whom were steeped in calligraphical history. But in his last years his friendship with Morison was frequently punctuated by attacks against his friend's programme of type revivals, and also against his attitude towards the relative importance that should be given in type design to *engraving* as distinct from *calligraphy*. Both men enjoyed an argument, and enjoyed it still more if it took place after a good meal with fine wines. I was not present on those occasions, but Morison's views have happily been preserved in a characteristic letter written on 5 March 1956 from which Van Krimpen quoted extensively – but neither *in toto* nor with complete accuracy – when he wrote his Typophile Chap Book *On Designing and Devising Type* (1957).

What prompted Morison to write that letter was the arrival of a lengthy memorandum compiled by Van Krimpen some three months after the Hofer manuscript. It had the cumbersome title 'On preparing designs for Monotype faces so as to prevent arbitrary encroachments from the side of the drawing office on the designer's work and intentions and otherwise inevitable disappointments at the designer's end'. Copies were sent, on 1st March 1956, to me and to a few others at the Monotype Corporation. The memorandum repeated in similar terms many of the observations made in the Hofer manuscript, on which I comment below. But here I draw attention to the fact that as early as May 1956, while Van Krimpen was on holiday in Italy, he began to make notes for the Typophile Chap Book. That book was clearly influenced by Morison's letter of 5 March 1956, which in turn was provoked by Van Krimpen's two lengthy essays – the Hofer manuscript (November 1955) and the Monotype memorandum (March 1956).

Exactly how many times Van Krimpen broke into print during his last years can be seen in the select handlist on pp.95–6, I need not refer to him again as a writer before I turn to the contents of the Hofer manuscript. But I must still give a brief explanation of Van Krimpen's own methods as a *designer* (as distinct from a writer) *of letters*. He made drawings for all his types on a hard, heavily-sized sheet of paper. This had rather a rough surface which, he said, gave him a good grip on the paper. Despite its surface, he was still able to make highly-finished designs upon it in one large size, approximately two inches high. Nearly all his designs were then interpreted by an extremely skilled punch-cutter, who cut punches in every size for which types were required. Part of the punchcutter's art is to make the small but important adjustments which *must* be made to a basic design if it is to serve for a whole range of sizes, from the size of the smallest footnote to the largest display line.

Van Krimpen was fortunate to have had the collaboration of a punchcutter of exceptional skill, employed in the typefoundry of Enschedé en Zonen. His name was P.H.Rädisch, and he had learnt his craft at the Reichsdruckerei in Berlin. By frequent contacts between these two men, a team of unusual effectiveness was built up. All the types produced at Enschedé from Van Krimpen's designs were cut by Rädisch, but Van Krimpen seldom mentioned his name. Not even when he discussed this matter in a posthumously printed essay 'A Perspective on Type and Typography' did he give the name of his punchcutter. Instead he argued the principle in his habitual and somewhat circuitous fashion, saying first that he was rather in favour 'when names are being mentioned at all, of not concealing the punchcutter's name'. But he then went on to claim that as the designer works with the technically skilled hands and eyes of his punchcutter, the latter can be replaced without noticeable difference in the result. The cooperation comes to an end with the disappearance of the designer, but not with that of the punchcutter. 'Consequently', concluded Van Krimpen, 'I can understand the opinion that there is no need to mention this auxiliary hand's name'.

The name of Rädisch is not mentioned in the Typophile Chap Book *On Designing and Devising Type* (1957), but on the last page of that book Van Krimpen wrote: 'What are designs without the finished product? As an answer to this rhetorical question, I want to pay tribute to the punchcutter of the House of Enschedé...; without his zeal and skill my designs could hardly have become the printing material they are'.

Van Krimpen's enforced reliance upon another man's skill in order to make his own designs into printing material gave rise to the philosophical doubts which make his views expressed in the Hofer manuscript of particular interest. These doubts were accentuated when later he was forced to rely upon the skill of the Type Drawing Office staff and engineers of the Monotype Corporation, and finally upon the Lumitype studio personnel in Paris.

RÉSUMÉ OF THE HOFER MANUSCRIPT

At this point I introduce my résumé of the Hofer manuscript. Every reader should read the entire manuscript (reproduced in facsimile on pp. 47–87), but having done so, it may be helpful to read the following résumé before the commentary which follows:

(1–5) Words cannot force acceptance of a design which is not visually acceptable. So Van Krimpen declines Hofer's request to write about his own type designs, but instead turns to the subject given in his title.

(6) The creation of punches and matrices, by machine, instead of by hand, creates new problems. (7) Van Krimpen believes hand-cut punches are the best but (8) mechanical methods are unavoidable and indispensable for mechanically printed books, newspapers and periodicals.

(8–9) Various other writers have written about the defects of mechanical punchcutting. An observation by Lewis and Brinkley is quoted: 'The pantograph punchcutting machine only produces a dehumanized version of what may have been a sprightly original'. (10) Van Krimpen considers their observation correct, but denies their right to reach their 'too generalizing and hopeless, conclusion'.

(11–13) Updike noted that pantographic punchcutting 'tended to mechanize the design of type' and in particular when one design was used for all sizes of a series (whereas a new model *ought* to be made for every two sizes of type). (12) Updike is praised by Van Krimpen for his perspicacity but criticized for saying 'it is only when a machine is as flexible as the hand that it is as good as the hand'.

(12–13) *Pace* Van Krimpen, 'hand & machine are two different tools from which fundamentally different achievements should be asked'.

(14–15) He asserts that the pantographic punchcutting machine can be made to produce a counterpart of any sprightly original, but he considers that it is wrong to make such use of the machine. He holds that it is dishonest to use a machine to imitate hand-work. (16) He concedes that others may not be interested in his philosophy of handicraft as against mechanical work, but he maintains that those slight irregularities which the human eye and hand always leave in manual work are an important part of the charm of type for which the punches were cut by hand. In machine-made types these irregularities cannot wholly be compensated by those few and insignificant blemishes which cannot be avoided, even by the most careful operation of machines.

(18) Van Krimpen disagrees with Bruce Rogers' approval of the machine-cut patterns made by Wiebking for Centaur.

(19) Van Krimpen fails to discover in Stanley Morison's *A Tally of Types* that the problems of punchcutting treated in Van Krimpen's essay were ever of interest to Morison. (20) He is not convinced by Morison's assertion that 'the way to learn to go forward was to make a step backward' and disagrees with much of what Morison caused to be recut, despite his high regard for Morison's achievements with the Monotype Corporation from 1922 to 1932. (22–24) He is especially critical of Monotype Poliphilus,

but wholeheartedly agrees with Morison's comment that it was 'accurate without realizing the intention of the original'. (25) He claims that Morison evidently shared his views because he wrote of the romans Jannon reproduced that they were remarkable in quality but 'cannot be said to yield anything like a close facsimile'. He quotes a similar criticism by Harry Carter of Monotype Fournier for preserving little of the character of the original.

(27) Van Krimpen then quotes Bruce Rogers who believed 'perhaps only hand-cut punches, cut by the designer of the type, can preserve the real feeling of the design'. He questions whether we can be sure that Aldus and Jenson engraved their own types, and finds fault in some of the punches cut by Claude Garamont.

(28) He thinks there is a lot to be said for 'close collaboration between one man specializing in designing types and another in engraving the punches'. (29) He maintains that there are three stages in drawing a design for a typeface. (31) First a drawing in erasable and easily corrected form, not too precise or exact. Second in pencil, leaving little to guess. Third as near as the designer can make it, drawn in carbon ink. (31–32) He notes that generally draughtsmen working for punchcutting machines do not make filled-in drawings, but large scale, reversed drawings in outline only. (33) He appends drawings which exemplify these three stages, and notes that the second and third stages are progressively less satisfactory. This leads him to conclude that the faults attributed by Lewis and Brinkley to the punchcutting machine are in fact to be found in drawings made by draughts- men for such machines. So Van Krimpen would prefer to have the punchcutter work from drawings in the first stage, provided that there is sufficiently close cooperation between designer and

punchcutter. (35) Because so much has been lost by the third stage drawing, he does not wish to use it for any practical working purpose.

(35–36) Van Krimpen declares that a good designer who is an able punchcutter himself, will make good, maybe the best possible, work. But if a good designer works in close collaboration with a good punchcutter, they may produce equally good things, and they will show the characteristic advantages of the work of human hands. (36–37) Fundamentally he agrees with Updike that the punchcutting machine tends to mechanize type design. For being a machine, what else can it do? Perhaps Updike meant to say that the machine actually had a mechanizing influence on the design itself.

(38) As to the second stage drawing, this is the one that Van Krimpen would like to see used as a model by the type drawing office, in the stage preceding the mechanical cutting of the punches. Such drawings must be as perfect as possible and free of any signs that betray the hand, and so would yield a true machine-made type. He does not know if the results would be satisfactory, but in their austerely mechanical appearance they would have achieved the human virtue of honesty which he seeks.

THE ROLE OF THE PUNCHCUTTER

In view of his repeated remarks about honesty in making types, I am surprised that Van Krimpen did not dwell at length on the virtues of designing a type in the actual size in which it is to be used. For it cannot be denied that only a designer-punchcutter can produce a completely *honest* type, in Van Krimpen's sense of the word. By working with gravers and files in the true scale, a punchcutter is enabled to produce types so small that no designer could draw them in such sizes with either pens or brushes. And if a designer is unable to make his designs in the actual sizes in which a type is to be made, he creates severe problems for the 'auxiliary' who is to interpret those designs. Eric Gill was well aware of this problem: 'It is difficult enough', he wrote in his *Essay on Typography* (1931), 'for the designer to draw a letter ten or twenty times as large as the actual type will be and at the same time in right proportion; it requires very great experience and understanding. It is quite impossible for a set of more or less tame employees... to know what a letter enlarged a hundred times will look like when reduced to the size of the intended type'. For this reason Gill also was of the opinion 'if the punch-cutter and the designer are the same person, so much the better'.

The late Victor Hammer was just such a rare combination of artist and craftsman. He chose to make types of an uncial character: it is of no consequence in this context to debate whether or not these particular types are judged to be successes or failures. Their virtue is that they wholly realised Hammer's intentions with that quality of honesty which was so dear to Van Krimpen. Hammer had little respect for the pantographic punchcutting machine and was caustic about Gill's readiness to have his types produced by such a machine. He said succinctly: 'It engraves punches, and matrices as well. But since there is no craftsman, the machine calls for a 'designer' and an 'operator'. – Well, now you have a machine which cannot see and a designer who cannot carve: so he prepares an enlarged drawing of a letter – the design'.

The absence of the craftsman was a serious matter to Hammer because as he saw it, 'the secret of the craftsman's procedure is

23

always to see details and distinctions in connection with the whole form he works upon. He does not know beforehand exactly what his work will look like – he will only know when he has finished it. No drawn or lettered 'design' can do else than anticipate what the punchcutter's hand and eye will produce'. Hammer went on to give an instance of how when he cut a punch for an 'o', he looked at the inner form of the left curve while working on the outer form of the right curve, and vice versa.

There are few men alive today who have engraved punches for types of their own design, and who have also designed types to be engraved mechanically. One such man is Sem Hartz, for many years a friend and colleague of Van Krimpen at Enschedé en Zonen. Hartz believes that when a type is designed for mechanical punchcutting, 'nothing should be left to the correcting influence of tools or material and to that feeling of fitness-for-purpose which the craftsman applies almost without being aware that he does so.... Type cut by hand, whether by the designer alone or by designer and punchcutter in close collaboration, may well have qualities lacking in a mechanically-cut type. Nevertheless there are many examples of mechanically-cut type designed by a master which surpass in quality many so-called types that are merely written or drawn letters imitated in steel or some other material'.

Much depends upon how the master who has designed a type controls the mechanics who produce it. The most prolific contemporary type designer, Hermann Zapf, has written whimsically of the battles which a type designer must be ready to fight with the mechanics: 'It is now a dogged tussle over form, the designer on the one side armed only with pencil and pen, and on the other his numerically superior opponents, fully mechanized and equipped with machines of utmost refinement. Woe, if the machine wins out and the characters are shaped after its judgment! Who will then need to wonder if the emergent letter is cold and soulless'?

In 1958 Stanley Morison gave a lecture to the Art Workers Guild in London in which he suggested that 'the quality of line obtainable by the hand of a skilled cutter of punches is *un*obtainable by any other man or means'. He went on to explain that 'engraving by hand is the only means by which typography can come into the possession and expression of a letter-form which is a direct and wholly human product. Moreover, the 'material shape' in question, as cut on the punch, and the quality of the cut-line made by the engraver of the punch (which is the exact size required for the text) are distinct from the quality of the pen-line made by the draughtsman of the diagram made on Bristol board, in a large size which is ultimately much reduced by pantograph to the size required by the text'.

Readers of the Hofer manuscript will have noted that Van Krimpen largely ignored the punchcutter's advantage, and indeed his responsibility, for creating a type in its true scale. Nor is there any mention in that manuscript of the uses of photography in designing types. Before Van Krimpen was even born, photography had been used by type designers. I now wish to turn to this subject.

USES OF PHOTOGRAPHY IN TYPE DESIGN

William Morris was, I believe, the first notable type designer to make systematic use of photography in preparing his designs for type. It was the sight of Emery Walker's photographic lantern slides of historic type, enlarged to a huge size in projection for his lecture at the New Gallery in 1888, that gave Morris both a taste and a technique for designing his own types. Emery Walker supplied him with photographic enlargements of fifteenth century types (a duplicate set is kept at the St Bride Printing Library in London). Morris then proceeded to draw his own designs on a similar large scale, but with a sound knowledge of how his drawings would relate to the size in which punches were to be cut by hand. By good fortune he was able to have his punches cut by the foremost punchcutter of his day, Edward Prince, whose interpretative skill was later applied to the execution of types drawn by Emery Walker's staff for the Doves and Cranach Presses, both of which originated from a close study of photographic enlargements of historic originals. In making the designs for the Doves type, Walker's craftsman drew over bleached-out prints of Jenson's fifteenth century types in an attempt to reconstitute this fine fount, for which the punches and matrices had long since vanished.

An attempt by Walker's draughtsman to copy a sixteenth century italic by the great writing master Tagliente was a failure because the would-be copier had too little understanding of Tagliente's style. To remedy this state of affairs, Emery Walker's patron, Count Harry Kessler, persuaded a pioneer in the revival of the art of calligraphy to supervise and correct the recutting of the Tagliente design. Edward Johnston achieved a considerable degree of success by making large-scale drawings and sketches for the guidance of the punchcutter–again it was Edward Prince. But before Prince began his work, he was provided with photographs of the drawings reduced to the scale in which he was to cut the punches. In this way, all of those concerned in the enterprise – printer, patron, scribe and punchcutter were able to examine an approximation of the intended type before work began on the punchcutting.

I use the word approximation because a photographic reduction cannot give a precisely accurate foretaste of the letters which the punches will serve to create. Johnston came to realise this when later he came to check the accuracy of Prince's successor, George Friend. What Johnston did was to have Friend's smoke proofs photographically enlarged to nine times their size, so that the prints corresponded in size with his original drawings: in this way he could determine how accurately or otherwise Friend had done his work. There followed a stream of detailed criticisms which Friend met with an admirable mixture of humility and commonsense: 'I will try to leave less room for complaint but the least bit out when magnified 9 times becomes a lot. The curves you point out in W M and V are practically impossible the size I am doing now: to do a curve to seem ever so little in the actual type, when enlarged would be too large according to the large photos of your drawing. I doubt if one person in a 100 would give me credit for meaning it'.

In my own experience, I have found that large-scale drawings for a set of small types can be a grave handicap to reaching a sound judgement, because there is a danger of becoming infatuated with subtle details which are only perceivable in the larger drawings, and which are quite irrelevant to the success of the type in its actual size. A type design must be judged in its true size, that is to say in the size in which it is to be manufactured for the purpose of being read. The expertise of those who manufacture types in their true size is an essential complement to the imagination and artistic skill of those who design letters on a large scale.

Eric Gill, one of Johnston's most successful pupils, made ingenious use of photographic enlargements for at least one of his type designs. Before he drew the letters for the Golden Cockerel type, he studied enlarged prints of three types. Next he made rough drawings, with an ordinary pen, in a size close to the 18-point in which it was first cut. His rough drawings were then enlarged photographically to the same scale as the enlarged prints of the three types he had already examined. Finally he made carefully finished drawings upon enlarged bleached-out prints of his rough drawings. By this technique, Gill was able to conceive the type in its true scale at the time he made his first rough drawings. Furthermore, he was able to execute his final finished drawings upon prints enlarged to such a size that he could work upon them with the same pens and brushes he normally handled when he drew large designs for inscriptions.

As was to be expected of a man who *cut* letters, Gill was acutely aware of the difference between a drawn and a cut letter. So when he produced his first sketches for a display type named Jubilee, he actually cut the letters out of a sheet of cardboard, and then placed this sheet upon a blackened piece of pasteboard, so that the cut letters stood out clearly. By this technique he was able to simulate, on an enlarged scale, the effect of a cut letter.

Unlike Van Krimpen, Gill had a sound training and experience both of writing and of cutting letters with his own hands. Van Krimpen was only able to draw letters, he never cut them with his own hands in any medium – wood, metal or stone – although he did produce designs for a number of fine pieces of engraved letters. In my view this partly accounts for the circuitous arguments in which he often engaged Morison concerning the relative importance to be given in type design to calligraphy and engraving.

At a critical point in the Hofer manuscript, Van Krimpen wrote: 'Not everybody can or will think of the same things; they may not be interested in my philosophy of handicraft as against mechanical work;– and, after all, my philosophy may be ridiculous if not nonsensical (though I am not prepared to admit this as long as no better arguments are opposed to mine)'.

His arguments can be summed up thus: an object should be made in accordance with the nature of the tool used to make it. It is, he maintains, senseless to imitate the work of a machine by hand, and it is dishonest to imitate by means of a machine what has first been made by hand. He restated his opinion with greater clarity in a letter written to Morison on 15 March 1956: 'Work done by hand and mechanical products are two fundamentally differents things. We should never forget that and we should let them remain different: the one makes things; for the other designs have to be made'.

The last phrase echoes the remark by Victor Hammer quoted on p. 23, for he similarly noted the need to provide for the machine a designer and an operator. Another quotation from Hammer compresses into twenty-two words a belief which seems to have exerted a dominant influence on Van Krimpen's philosophy. Here, then, is Hammer's definition of 'the "mystical" quality of handiwork: it is that trace of life which lingers on in things made entirely by the human hand'.

Hammer's definition clarifies Van Krimpen's viewpoint, and to the extent that both men place a special value on handicraft, I agree with them. But at the point where Van Krimpen refers to the mechanical cutting of punches, I maintain that he exaggerates in claiming that there are *fundamental* differences between cutting punches by hand and by machine. The differences are in my view technical, rather than fundamental. Furthermore, I consider that both men underestimated the importance of human hands and intelligence both in devising and constructing machines, and in operating them. In my experience, type designs can be either improved or adulterated by the use of machines, according to the skill and experience of the persons who operate the machines. Indisputably, certain makes of typesetting machines have inherent limitations which have to be respected by those who cut punches mechanically to serve particular machines. Type made by a typefounder can subsequently be rubbed down so as to produce a tighter fit (that is to say, a lesser degree of space between letters) than is possible with any mechanical typesetting machine which casts in metal. But when it comes to the effect of machinery on the design of printing types, I can cite one passage in which Van Krimpen acknowledges that for certain categories of types, the design can actually be cut more satisfactorily by machine than by hand.

In discussing the series of sans serifs which he made for Romulus, Van Krimpen wrote in his Typophile Chap Book: 'There can be no better means than the intelligently conducted engraving machine to de-individualize the subtle personal variations which may be quite as well discernable in sans serif as in any other typeface. In my sans serifs, which have never reached the stage of being cut by machine, they are there as the hand of the punch-cutter made them. In the hand-cut version they are numerous and obvious. It should have been the machine's job to leave them as numerous as they are but, by mechanizing them, to reduce their obviousness'. I would hate to have been the overseer who had to explain to those responsible for making patterns for the punchcutting machine, and also to those who operated the punchcutting machine, just how they were to interpret Van Krimpen's desire to leave the personal variations in his original designs as numerous as they were but nevertheless to mechanize them to reduce their obviousness. Nor can I understand why Van Krimpen, who did not scorn the use of French curves when he drew his designs, should have considered it right and proper to leave it to another mind 'and another set of hands' to make decisions which many designers consider to be their own rightful responsibility. And after considering Van Krimpen's remarks about the interpretation of his own sans serif designs by mechanical punchcutting, I am unable to reconcile it with the last sentence but one in the Hofer manuscript, in which he claims that a type would have the human virtue of honesty by its 'austerely mechanical appearance'. If an austerely mechanical appearance is considered to be such cardinal virtue, is it honest to give orders that a machine is to leave personal variations as numerous as they were in a designer's drawing? I share the view held on this subject by Sem Hartz (see p.24) and I therefore consider that it is dishonest, and impracticable, to give such orders.

POLIPHILUS AND OTHER TYPE REVIVALS

Although it will be evident that I have little sympathy for many of Van Krimpen's philosophical objections, I fully understand his objections to Monotype Poliphilus. There was an element of the mock antique about this type which was absent from the other revivals of historic types cut at Morison's instigation by the Monotype Corporation. It was of course very easy for Van

Krimpen to be wise in 1955 about the events of 1923; but it should be remembered that in the early nineteen-twenties there was a widespread desire to show that even the trained eye could not tell the difference between hand composition and mechanical typesetting. It therefore became important to show that type cut and cast by hand could not be distinguished from type produced by mechanical means.

The reader can read Morison's reply to some of Van Krimpen's criticisms of Poliphilus in his letter of 5 March 1956 printed as Appendix 1. But it is only fair to refer as well to Morison's own criticisms of Poliphilus made in *A Tally of Types* (Cambridge 1953). In that book, of which a new edition is announced for publication in 1972, Morison explained that Harry Lawrence first put forward the idea of recutting the Poliphilus type, which he intended to use for a type-facsimile edition of *The Dream of Polifilo*. Even after that plan was abandoned, the making of the type went ahead, using as a model some sheets of the original 1499 edition supplied by Lawrence.

As Morison put it: 'To redraw, and not merely reproduce, an ancient original, available only in the form of a contemporary print, was a more difficult art than direct imitation; and this was what Rogers had accomplished with his Centaur. But the Corporation had not in 1923 the experience gained later'. After admitting that the Monotype recutting of Poliphilus was not perfect in point of reproduction technique, he expressed his regret that 'due care was not taken in 1923 to find the best pages for the reconstruction and the reproduction of the fount instead of relying upon the sheets provided by Lawrence. The original 1499 edition varies notably from page to page. Some sections of the book are printed from sparkling new, others from soft and

old, type. Unfortunately, the leaves presented to the Corporation by Lawrence were detached from the less well-printed
portions. In the result, the recutting lacks the grace of the type
as it appeared in its earliest cutting'.

Close examination of Poliphilus and its accompanying italic,
Blado, will show that the work was open to a far graver objection
than is suggested by Morison's mention of the difference between
sparkling new and soft old type. For in several characters it will be
seen that the punches cut by the Monotype Corporation went so
far as to embody the uneven inkspread made when the letters
were originally impressed into dampened hand-made paper.
The italic capital W is a particularly grievous example of this
error of judgement.

I therefore consider that Van Krimpen had good reason to
attack the recutting of Poliphilus. But he makes clear in the
Hofer manuscript and in several other pieces written shortly
afterwards that he disapproved in principle of type revivals.
First he criticized Poliphilus with reason for being too slavish a
copy for satisfactory modern usage. Next he attacked Monotype
Fournier because it departed too much from its original pattern,
although these departures were made precisely so that the recutting should be more suitable for modern printing techniques.
In designing the Monotype versions of Bembo and Baskerville,
similar adjustments were successfully made. But Van Krimpen
would have none of it, and in his memorandum to the Monotype
Corporation written a few months after he had completed the
Hofer manuscript he wrote: 'I have called these pretending copies
of ancient typefaces neither flesh nor fish...they are given a look
of being handiwork, in as much [as] they follow painstakingly the
engraver's and even the typefounder's irregularities'. And this

again he did not hesitate 'to call – but may it be well understood: philosophically speaking – *dishonesty*'. His attack would have impressed me the more if he had distinguished between those revivals which were *painstakingly* done in a mistaken way, and those which were judicious interpretations of historic designs which deliberately departed in detail from the originals in order to make them revivals more suitable for mechanical use.

It is relevant to conclude this section with some remarks on Monotype Bembo recently expressed by Dr Giovanni Mardersteig, who had first hand experience of the difficulties of basing a type for current use on the model of the types originally cut by Francesco Griffo, known to us from the first printing of Cardinal Bembo's tract *De Aetna* (1495). Dr Mardersteig's opinion is that 'the weight of Monotype Bembo is much more even than Griffo's cutting, and it has the advantage of being more suitable for general use because of its deviations from the original model, some of them made for technical reasons and others in order to produce a more regular appearance. Although it cannot be denied that the hand of Griffo can no longer be readily detected in the Monotype version, the type is nevertheless freer from idiosyncracy and more modern, without completely abandoning the characteristics of the model upon which it was based'.

THE MICHELANGELO ANALOGY

Van Krimpen's digression on the differing qualities of two pieces of sculpture by Michelangelo does little to strengthen his arguments. Both the sculptures illustrated are works of fine art, not of applied art. Van Krimpen realized the weakness of citing such works in an essay devoted to the mechanical cutting of punches:

this much is clear from his otherwise obscure comment 'I will of course not say that the difference of class between sculpture and type design is not maintained never to be forgotten'. Presumably he was merely trying to explain that in works of fine art, as well as in type designs, he preferred results free of too high a finish; and that above all he looked for results which remained 'characteristically the work of human hands', even if (as is the case with types) they had to be produced partly by mechanical methods.

VAN KRIMPEN'S THREE DRAWINGS

Drawings of five characters in three different stages of completion were included in the Hofer manuscript, and they are reproduced together on p.92. It is common practice for a type designer to go through the three stages indicated, but unusual for the earlier states of a drawing to be preserved. What is still more unusual is for a designer to admit that he regrets the need to commit himself to the final precise stage of a drawing. Yet it will quickly be perceived on examining the three states of the 'g' that the ambiguities of weight in the outline drawings drawn by pencil confer a pleasing quality which is lacking in the unambiguous filled-in final drawing. (The reader should look closely at the differences in the 'ear' of the letter 'g'.)

Van Krimpen hoped to transfer from the skilled punchcutter to the 'drawing office' some of the interpretative skills upon which he had become so dependent. The drawing office was of vital importance because it produced the patterns which guided the operation of punchcutting machines. A really skilled drawing office might work satisfactorily from the second stage drawing. But in future, for reasons which I explain in the final paragraph of this introduction, highly finished drawings will be required of type designers for the reproduction of types by photographic methods.

VAN KRIMPEN'S VIEWS CONTRASTED WITH THOSE OF BRUCE ROGERS

Van Krimpen and Bruce Rogers shared a high regard for each other's work, both as type designers and as book designers. Because Van Krimpen does not give the full text in the Hofer manuscript of the citation (made by Updike in his *Printing Types* vol. I, pp. II–I2) of Rogers' comments upon mechanical punch-cutting, I will now print the passage *in extenso:* 'Even with strict instructions and with best intentions,' wrote Rogers, 'it is difficult for the habitual user of a very accurate machine *not* to insensibly smooth out what he has always been taught to consider "imperfections" and to make as mechanically perfect a letter as possible... I have come to believe that perhaps only hand-cut punches, *cut by the designer of the type*, can preserve the real feeling of the design'; and having concluded his citation of Rogers' own words, Updike wrote 'and he adds that the design should be drawn as nearly as possible to the exact size of the desired font'.

The Carl H. Pforzheimer Library in New York contains an unpublished and undated notebook in the hand of Bruce Rogers, which he labelled 'Bye-Ways of Book-making, or, Random Notes of a Tramp Printer'. Its opening sentences admit that the machine is capable of higher achievements than Rogers was prepared to concede in the passage quoted above. 'Beautiful types can be cut by machine as well as by hand – but not if a machine, *or a machinist,* designs them. Our modern types all look too professional – too skilfully made. When we have seen the details of one letter, we know what similar details of all the other letters will be. Whereas in a really fine type there are perpetual variations, within narrow limits it is true, but still enough to give a living quality to the type when combined into words. The chief interest in such types as the Fell type is the avoidance of the professional appearance – otherwise they have few positive merits. But the designer must be careful how he goes about getting this irregularity. A studied negligence must not be overdone. It should look as though attained unconsciously'.

I have no reason to believe that Van Krimpen ever saw the notebook from which the last quotation is taken; if he had read it, he would no doubt have been prompted to say more harsh things about the dishonesty of using a machine to produce a type that could deceive the eye into assuming it had been made by hand. Nevertheless, even if we ignore the highly personal interpretation which Van Krimpen gave to the word honesty in this context, it must not be overlooked that whereas Rogers uses the adjective *accurate* to describe the quality of the machine, Van Krimpen uses the adverb *slavishly* to castigate its use. In one sentence Van Krimpen admits that a machine-cut version of Rogers' Centaur type is charming, yet still protests that this charming result has been dishonestly achieved.

INCONSISTENCIES IN VAN KRIMPEN'S VIEWS

In fact Van Krimpen wanted to have it both ways. He wanted the operator of punchcutting machinery to produce a result which was accurate up to a point, but interpretative to an important degree: he specifically desired the operator, in executing a design, to do away with 'the slightest irregularities, left in it by the designer's hand', but at the same time insisted that the original design contained 'its characteristic lines, to be slavishly followed in the working drawing'. In my view, this too could be considered a dishonest use of machinery – the essential characteristic of which is its *accuracy*. Rogers held that it was the designer's job to produce a charming design which would subsequently be accurately manufactured by mechanical means, whereas Van Krimpen, long used to the incomparable advantage of working with another craftsman, hankered after a solution which would preserve the advantage of a punchcutter's interpretative skill with the unrivalled accuracy and perfection of a machine-made article.

FUTURE USES OF MECHANICAL METHODS IN MAKING TYPES

Within a few months of completing the Hofer manuscript, Van Krimpen wrote: 'Cutting punches by machine is still young; younger men will find where it is wrong and will direct it in the right way in due time'. I fully agree with the spirit of this remark, but not with the terms in which it was couched. Mechanical punchcutting is fast declining as a technique for manufacturing type designs. The majority of new types are now reproduced by two-dimensional photographic masters, not by three-dimensional punches. The actual techniques used vary considerably in detail, but they all share one great advantage. As soon as the photographic masters have been made, a designer can obtain proofs of his type in a wide range of sizes. Next to working in the actual size in which a type is to be made, the best solution is for a designer to concentrate quickly upon such proofs of his types in their true sizes. The original drawing is merely a means to an end. It is unhelpful and unhealthy for a type designer to become obsessed with any minutiae of design which are visible only in large-scale original drawings but invisible, and often irrelevant, in the sizes of the finished types.

VAN KRIMPEN'S ESSAY IN RELATION TO HIS LIFE AND WORK

The Hofer manuscript was written three years before Van Krimpen's death. During his last years, he was disgruntled for a variety of reasons. He was in poor health and his private life was in turmoil. He was at loggerheads with several of his friends and colleagues. He was disenchanted with much of his own work, including his entrancingly graceful *cancellaresca bastarda*, a type which has lately been used to great effect by private press printers such as Raymond Gid in France, and Leonard Baskin in the U.S.A.

Many of the arguments he put forward in the Hofer manuscript were poorly developed; he had failed to maintain some of them in discussion with Morison and Hartz, and had chosen to ignore many of the counter-arguments put forward by other experts with first hand knowledge of type design.

The reasons for printing his Hofer manuscript in facsimile are twofold. First, it provides a handsome specimen of his calligraphy for those who are only familiar with his fine range of original type designs. Second, his essay raises a number of fundamental issues important to anybody who is concerned with making type designs. By clarifying these issues, I hope that readers may find it profitable to study the contents, and not merely the form, of the Hofer manuscript.

I would have been unwilling to level so many criticisms against the arguments of a dead friend if I had not already written a book which paid tribute to his creative work as a designer. My admiration is undiminished for Van Krimpen as a type designer, typographer, calligrapher, and designer of inscriptions, stamps and other objects in which lettering played a prominent part. His formidable achievements as a creative artist will ensure his enduring reputation.

To end, I will quote a sentence written in a visitors book by Rudolf Koch, a great German type designer. His words movingly explain why men such as he and Van Krimpen devoted a lifetime to the design of letters. 'The making of letters in every form is for me the purest and the greatest pleasure, and at many stages of my life it was to me what a song is to the singer, a picture to the painter, a shout to the elated, or a sigh to the oppressed – it was and is for me the most happy and perfect expression of my life'.

JOHN DREYFUS

ACKNOWLEDGEMENTS

Miss Heather Child, Mr. Matthew Carter and Mr. Sem Hartz made valuable comments and suggestions for which I wish to make special acknowledgement. I also wish to express my gratitude to Mr. Huib Van Krimpen for permission to print his father's manuscript, as well as to The Monotype Corporation and the literary executors of Stanley Morison for permission to reproduce the letter on pp. 97–101.

SELECT BIBLIOGRAPHY

CARTER, HARRY 'Letter Design and Typecutting', pp. 878–95 in the *Journal of the Royal Society of Arts*, no. 4935, vol. CII (London, 1954).

DREYFUS, JOHN *Italic Quartet: a record of the collaboration between Harry Kessler, Edward Johnston, Emery Walker and Edward Prince in making the Cranach Press Italic* (Cambridge, privately printed, 1966).

– 'George Friend 1881–1969: a Memoir', pp. 81–6 in the *Journal of the Printing Historical Society*, no. 5 (London, 1969).

GILL, ERIC *An Essay on Typography*, especially pp. 77 and 81 (London, Sheed & Ward, 1931).

HAMMER, VICTOR 'Digressions on the Roman Letter', pp. 25–38 in *Chapters on Writing and Printing* (Lexington, The Anvil Press, 1963).

– *Memory and Her Nine Daughters, The Muses, a Pretext for Printing, Cast into the Mould of a Dialogue in Four Chapters*, p. 75 (New York, George Wittenborn Inc., 1957).

HARTZ, S. L. 'An Approach to Type Designing', pp. 39–42 in *Penrose Annual*, vol. 52 (London, 1958).

MARDERSTEIG, GIOVANNI *De Aetna Liber & Pietro Bembo on Etna* (Verona, Officina Bodoni, 1969), see especially pp. 139–40.

MORISON, STANLEY review of 'The Treyford Type', pp. 180–5 in *The Fleuron*, no. VII (Cambridge University Press and Doubleday Doran & Co., 1930).

– *A Tally of Types cut for Machine Composition and introduced at the University Press, Cambridge* (Cambridge, privately printed, 1953).

– *Typographic Design in Relation to Photographic Composition*, with an introduction by John Carter (San Francisco, The Book Club of California, 1959).

ROGERS, BRUCE *The Centaur Types* (Chicago, October House, 1949).

– 'Bye-Ways of Book-making, or Random Notes of a Tramp Printer', an unpublished manuscript in the Carl H. Pforzheimer Library, New York.

– See also Updike who quotes Rogers in *Printing Types* cited below.

UPDIKE, D. B. *Printing Types: Their History, Forms and Use,* notably in vol. I, pp. 10–13 (Harvard University Press and Oxford University Press, 2 vols., 1922).

ZAPF, HERMANN *About Alphabets: Some Marginal Notes on Type Design,* translated by Paul Standard (New York, Typophile Chap Book no. XXXVII, 1960).

THE FACSIMILE

The facsimile on the following pages reproduces Harvard MS. TYP 410. The original manuscript measures 6⅞ x 9⅞ inches, and was written upon pale green paper made by Barcham Green, and was scored by Van Krimpen at intervals of ⅜ of an inch. It was written with Talens permanent blue ink using a no. 284 pen nib made by R. Esterbrook & Co. The manuscript was bound in blue buckram after it was accessioned by Harvard College Library.

For this manuscript Van Krimpen used a semi-formal italic cursive identical with that employed in all his personal and business correspondence. He was accustomed to write at great speed, and this is reflected in the grace and freedom which is characteristic of his hand. The influence of roman is apparent in his capitals and in his lower case g. Above and below the x-height of the lower-case letters, the ascenders and descenders rise and descend generously, and are occasionally allowed to intertwine. Serifs rarely appear on the letters, but some terminals end with a slight swelling or blob.

The letters are not unduly compressed and the inter-word spacing is generous. Separation between the letters is very good, and the upward strokes in *n* and letters of similar construction begin low, as they should. The writing is notable for the excellent relationship between the letters, and for the harmony between thick and thin strokes.

A LETTER to PHILIP HOFER
on certain problems connected with the
mechanical cutting of punches

Heemstede November 1955

Dear Philip: When you asked me to write on my own type faces I immediately had a feeling that I rather should not do it even if I may have consented readily enough; my compliance must have been due to a natural gift of persuasion of yours. I have changed my mind since; and I feel that I owe you some explanation on my changed attitude. I will therefore try to give you, in a kind of introduction, my reasons for thinking why people should not write on their own work if it can at all be avoided.

To me it seems obvious that explaining writing by further writing is a bit strange: why should an author not write at once in such a way that his works intelligibly explain themselves? But when it is done there can not be said that one medium is

1

called to the aid of an other medium. This happens when any other kind of work is accompanied by explanatory writing. And here, too, one is entitled to ask why the maker of the thing did not express himself distinctly in his freely chosen medium.

Even if one thinks that there is an undeniable difference of class between painting or composing music, on the one hand, and making glasses or designing type, on the other, it is still permissible to make certain comparisons between those arts and these crafts; always provided that the craftsman never loses sight of the difference of class and that he does not object to extending similar comparisons to, for instance, shoe making or cooking as well. It is a bit strange when an author wants to elucidate his writing by further writing; but there is

2

something wrong when a painter or a musician think it necessary to give an explanation in words of their painting or music: have not the makers failed if their works really need such dissertations? For should not these works be clear and intelligible on their own merits? Or, to put it in a slightly different way, will ever a commentator, be it the artist himself or somebody else, be able to make, by force of words, a work of art acceptable that is not already acceptable as it stands? The only reasonable comment that artist or craftsman may give to their work is, to my mind, a title which will be the better the less pretentious it sounds. If this, together with the work itself, will not do I feel almost certain that nothing will. If a musician is content to call his composition symphony, divertimento or concerto

3

grosso, I feel better at ease than when he gives it some ornate literary title. (Though I must, by way of digression, at once add that there exist many fine pieces of music which do have such names; but, then, they may have been invented after the music itself had been written and they are, in many instances, nothing but a matter of fashion.)

The same applies to glasses or type & to any other craftman's achievements which are not art per se. There is nothing that a maker of glasses should defend to say that he has made some particular glass for claret or certain others for brandy or for beer. And, likewise, a designer of printing types has the right, if not the duty, to inform the printing trade that this or that type face is meant for newspaper work or an

4

other one for poetry or for novels. It is for his fellow typographers, and for printers and publishers, to decide whether they want to use his designs at all; and, if yes, for which purpose. It is to them, too, to weigh the merits of any given design. It has to be taken for granted that its maker has done all he could do in wrestling with the familiar and yet so rebellious forms of the letters & to reconcile his design with the limitations which both typefounding and mechanical composition, in their several ways, impose. I repeat my question whether it is imaginable that a design which is not acceptable as it stands could be made acceptable by force of words. — I strongly feel that it is, or at least should be, thus. I therefore do not want to comment on my, I am afraid, too numerous designs.

I can now come to the problems mentioned in the title I have given to this letter. They came, unnoticed at the beginning, into existence when punches and matrices were first being made mechanically instead of by hand. These problems have been haunting me for many years already. I so far do not see a solution for them; and I am not in the least certain — though not, believe me, from some arrogant feeling that if I do not see it it can not be seen by anybody — that there is or can be found one at all. Maybe I am wrong, and there are several remedies, but I even fail to see in which direction to look for a single one. If I may succeed in making clear what I mean I shall already feel that I have not written entirely in vain.

There has been a beginning of decline in the craft and trade of making printing types before any engraving machine came into use. I am thinking of the practice— which, by the way, has never been general— of making matrices by way of electro deposit. It means that punches are not really punches, of steel or at least of a harder metal than the matrices struck or driven from them, but just letters fashioned in an alloy too soft and too easy to handle and, as a consequence, necessarily lacking the crispness peculiar to engraved steel.

My learned and wise friend Harry Carter and I agree in the opinion that, whatsoever technical and commercial people connected with typefoundries or factories of composing machines may think or say, still the best and most reliable way of making printing type is by means of steel punches, cut by hand, and struck or driven matrices. At the same time, however, we understand perfectly well that with the present methods of making books, not even to speak of periodicals and newspapers, composing machines and from beginning to end mechanically produced printing type are unavoidable and indispensable. We shall therefore have to put up with them & whilst doing so, to try and find out how we can meet with their problems and avoid their defects.

I have by no means been the first to detect that there is something wrong. I think it a remarkable fact that Updike, who as far as I know never has actually been a typefounder, comes (in Printing Types I pages 10–14) so much nearer to the core and essence of the matter than any of his contemporaries or, at that, of younger writers.

Of others I will only deal with two; besides quoting by the bye the opinion of two of the youngest authors who give this opinion rather apodictically, too apodictically perhaps, & who seem to take it for granted that no remedy for the trouble they have noticed is possible. Perhaps their attitude bears witness of more wisdom than mine; but I am unable to resign myself as long as I hope that the right way of proceeding may be found.

John Lewis and John Brinkley (in Graphic Design, London 1954, page 111) say "The pantograph punch-cutting machine only produces a dehumanized version of what may have been a sprightly original." To this I say, to begin with, that if this should be the general opinion of people who are now in their forties there seems little hope of our escaping to go full speed towards a mechanized and

9

dehumanized "brave new world" that can
only be sweet to live in for such individuals,
if individuals there can still be spoken of,
as have not known a more humane world:
ramshackle and faulty though it may have
been. And, further, I must add that though
their observation seems, alas, all too correct
they hardly have a right to come to their, too
generalizing and hopeless, conclusion.

The other two authors — who, at the same
time, are practicians : the one of the generation
preceding my own and the other of about my
age — I have hinted at are Bruce Rogers
and Stanley Morison. They have both had,
quite recently, an opportunity to have their
say in the matter I am dealing with.
Bruce Rogers in The Centaur Types,
October House 1949, and Stanley Morison
in A Tally of Types, Cambridge 1953, &

10

it is remarkable that neither of them has seized his opportunity; from which I am afraid we have to infer that neither of them sees or feels the problems I am discussing as such.

Let me first sum up Updike's points which may show that, if he has done little or nothing to remedy the ailment, his diagnosis was very correct indeed.

He says—as you know his book is over thirty years old—that "today" all type is not cut by hand but that the theory of the pantograph was adapted, in the second quarter of the nineteenth century, to producing wood type. He then mentions Benton and his machine (which has been considerably developed and improved since) and points out that what seemed to be "a wholly admirable invention" in fact tended to

11

mechanize the design of type; & in particular
when one design was being used for all sizes
of a series. An authority, he says,—which
unfortunately he does not name—told him
that a new model design should be made
for every two sizes of type.—He, further on,
quotes from a letter by Bruce Rogers to him
some remarks on the desirability of what
are generally thought to be imperfections;
after which the designer of Monotype Centaur
advocates hand-cut punches cut by the
designer of the type.—Then Updike says
that of late there has been an improvement
in type cut by machine; and he is actually
going wrong when he remarks that "it is
only when a machine is as flexible as the
hand that it is as good as the hand".—
Maybe it was too early, or maybe Updike
was too old, to understand that hand &

12

machine are two different tools from which
fundamentally different achievements should
be asked. I am coming back to this.

But you and anybody else who might
care to read this letter I refer to the pages
in Updike's book I have mentioned.

Updike's merit lies, I think, more in his
having seen so early — in a time when the
Bentons and Pierponts, inventors or inventors
and improvers, still were the indisputed
masters and directors of the engraving machine
— that there was something, nay very much,
wrong than in what he points out as, in
his opinion, favourable developments or
in prescriptions for further improvement.
That, for instance, his observation that
"each size is a law unto itself" has become
obsolete — since nowadays all users of
engraving machines know and conform

13

themselves to it — is rather a note to his credit than anything else; whether this lesson has been learned from him or this truth been found independently.

Certain statements of his, of which I will point out one in particular, are to be taken cum grano salis (and I doubt whether, from my point of view, and in the trend of my reasoning, a grain will do). He says that "it is only when a machine is as flexible as the hand that it is as good as the hand". Is not the engraving machine as flexible as the hand? And is it not exactly there that the danger lurks?

The pantograph punch-cutting machine is able — that is: can be made — to produce the exact counterpart of any "sprightly original" (to use once more the words of Lewis and Brinkley); and particularly so

14

when there are no limitations imposed by
a unit system, as with the Monotype machine
—but even then it is, on certain conditions,
not altogether impossible—, or with the
Linotype machine's inability to cast over-
hangs. It is, however, my firm conviction
that neither an engraving machine nor any
other machine should be used in this way.
A thing should be done, an object made,
either by hand or by machine and in any
case in accordance with the nature of
(let me call it) the tool that is being used.
Trying to imitate the work of a machine
by hand is senseless and, since it is impossible, it is foolish besides; to imitate a work
of hand by machine is dishonest. (1 must
add here at once, for 1 do not want to be
misunderstood, that similar dishonesty
is no sin, and therefore no dishonesty in

15

the daily but only in the highest sense of
the word, when it is committed unconsciously and unintentionally. When a
man imitates a hand forged casserole,
with all its hammer-marks, by one blow
of some powerful forging machine he is
doubtless dishonest in every sense of the
word.)

But this does not mean that men like
Rogers or Morison who have had people
play with (flexible) engraving machines,
in order to get in type as nearly as possible what they were looking for, should
be dishonest at heart. Not everybody can
or will think of the same things; they may
not be interested in my philosophy of
handicraft as against mechanical work;
—and, after all, my philosophy may be
ridiculous if not nonsensical (though I

am not prepared to admit this as long as no better arguments are opposed to mine).

It seems likely that the slight irregularities, which the human eye and hand always leave in manual work, are an important element of the charm of hand-cut type. There is, in a few places, still being produced some type in the old-fashioned way. Where will the punchcutter who is working by hand be in another twenty-five years? Is he not likely to have vanished by then? And quite possibly the world will bewail the loss of one more handicraft in yet another quarter of a century. But if the craft is bound to die that same world shall have to do with the mechanical production of printing types and, for the taches de beauté which are so charming, with the utterly

17

few and insignificant blemishes the mechanical process, if conducted rightly, can not avoid
to remain in even its most careful achievements.

Now look what Rogers and Morison
have done.

On pages 17–61 of his little book on the
Centaur types, I have mentioned, he first
shows the engraver's patterns — they are, as
Rogers states, by "Robert Wiebking of Chicago,
for cutting on his machines"— and, from my
point of view, they are fundamentally and
exactly what they ought not to be. It is true
that the result, in type, is charming; but
this result has been reached (1 am sorry
having to repeat the nasty word again &
again) by dishonest means.—The Monotype
version of Centaur is not fundamentally
different from this one for composition by
hand — although its author may have

18

modified some oddities of his handiwork —
and so needs not being dealt with separately.
Will Updike, who has known the type and
must have seen the patterns, have been satis-
fied with the flexibility of Wiebking's machine?
In his criticism, quoted by Rogers, there is a
restriction that leaves room for doubt: "The
late D. B. Updike, in his monumental work
Printing Types, wrote: 'It appears to me
one of the best Roman founts yet designed
in America, and, of its kind, the best
anywhere.'" What Updike has wanted to
imply with the insertion "of its kind" we
are unlikely ever to know.

I have read, and re-read several times,
Morison's A Tally of Types and I have
been unable to find that the subject of this
letter should be even the slightest point to
him. This is made possible by the fact that

the whole of his argumentation is built
on what he is putting as an axiom, which
he does not even try to prove, while, at its
best, it might have passed as a theorem
needing the closest reasoned proof imaginable. Take away Euclid's first axiom, or
just try to replace it, and either your plani-
metric science will be wholly upset or you
get something contrary to reason which
it may be fun to play but impossible to
work with.

Morison's axiom, to be found on page
21 of his essay, reads: "The way to learn
to go forward was to make a step backward". This being written on what was
begun in 1922 one is inclined to ask
whether, from William Morris onwards,
no sufficient steps backward had been
made already; and, again, why no attempt

to a proof for this assertion is given. For
stating that "These were the convictions
with which the Monotype Corporation's new
programme was drafted in January 1922"
will hardly do as a justification of this
rather surprising dictum.

Here once more I have to be on my guard
against possible misunderstandings. It
is to be understood that I have the highest
regard and admiration for Morison's
achievements in and with the Monotype
Corporation during the years, 1922-1932,
he is limiting his tally of types to and
during later years; even if, as is the case,
I do not agree with much of what he has
caused to be done. But how dull and colour-
less the world would be if everybody agreed
with everybody on everything!

I have searched his little book for places

where my problems might be under discussion;
only to find that when Morison touches them
he does not seem to feel them as such and
that, moreover, he is rather on the side of
Rogers than on mine. Looking back, after
more than thirty years, at the cutting of
the Corporation's Polifilo he might have been
struck by the fact that he had never been more
remote from genuinely mechanial machine
work than on that occasion. Talking of the
result he says, on page 38, that "it was
possible, in fact, to compose, according to
the correct dimensions of the original, a
page of the Monotype version, place it side
by side with the original, and find no
difference except in paper. This test was in
fact made, and, naturally, it gave the
greatest satisfaction to the works." One
would expect a similar statement rather

from "the works" than from a man like Morison;
for, if there be any truth in it, this truth is at
the utmost very relative. "The works", an
institution of technical precision, may be
able to measure to perfection — which, in fact,
is their unescapable practice — but by dint
of having learned that they have so thor-
oughly neglected their naturale sense of
seeing that, to them, seeing means measuring
and inversely. What, then, to think of the
statement quoted, coming from Morison,
who, as long as I know him, has assured
me that he is not a technical man, nor
wants to be one, for, as he has always said,
Walter Lewis is right in his opinion that
the non-technical man will demand the
impossible and so get the best possible?
Or is it "the works'" opinion he is giving
to come to his own on the next page, 39,

23

where he says: "It [the reproduction] is accurate without realizing the intention of the original"? Here it is the trained and sensitive eye of the master that dictates the speech. Here too, however, he allows the opportunity to pass of saying that the same applies to every reproduction, be it manual or mechanical, because, in case of the former, the re-producer is coming in with his own heart and eye and hand, since he is not able to borrow those of his predecessor, and, of the latter, because the machine has neither heart nor eye nor hand and because so many measuring sticks and purely technical hands are coming between model and product that the model may have lost its life before the product comes into being.

That Morison is well aware of the truth of what I have said about manual reproduction is shown by a sentence on page 50 where he is dealing with the Monotype's so-called Garamond of 1923. He says there: "The quality of Jannon's reproduction of his chosen romans is remarkable, but it cannot be said to yield anything like a close facsimile." Again, alas, he fails to attach the obvious general conclusion to his subtle observation of a particular instance.

In order not to have all of the criticism come from me, and only from me, I should like to tell that on Monotype Fournier, according to A Tally of Types cut in 1925, Harry Carter has written, in the Biographical Note of his Fournier on Typefounding (London, 1930, page XXXIII), "Monotype 'Fournier', useful type as it may be, preserves little of the character of the original." This criticism is not further accounted for

25

but I know that the writer's opinion concurs with mine. (That not the happy owners of a copy of this scarce volume try to look up this sentence unless theirs, like mine, is one of the half dozen or so which are in the original state : in the published edition page XXXIII has been replaced and the quoted sentence deleted.)

So far about Morison who, if he had chosen to think and to write about the things I am dealing with here and now, might have taken a heavy burden from my mind and almost certainly would have done it better than I am able to.

As a transition to stating my own points, as far as there are left any, I have, for a last time to revert to Bruce Rogers and his opinion, quoted by Updike, on hand-cut punches. I, too, shall have to say a few words on them.

"I have come to believe", Rogers says, "that perhaps only hand-cut punches, cut by the designer of the type, can preserve the real feeling of the design." There can a lot be said about, and perhaps rather against than before, this opinion. It is true that Morison has never succeeded in arguing Rogers over from his predeliction for Jenson into a preference for Aldus; but, still, he will certainly not say that the type faces used by Aldus are but poor stuff. Did Aldus ever cut punches for the type he was using? And is it not obvious that Aldus's influence on his type faces must have made them what they are? But, on the other hand, is Rogers so absolutely certain, and can he be, that Jenson did his own engraving or all of it? And what about Arrighi, who is one of the other

27

masters revered by Rogers, or the engraver
of what he thinks to be a type of Spanish
origin (still shown in the 1768 Enschedé
specimen book) of which nothing is further
known? The great Claude Garamont, it
seems, did cut his own punches; but it is
only his romans that are so good that it
is preposterous to hope that it might be
possible to equal their virile elegance.
His famous Grec du Roy, however, I can
only see, unsurpassedly elegant though
it may be, as a glorious failure.
   Is there not a lot to be said before a
close collaboration between one man specializing in designing types and another in
engraving the punches? I think there is; &
I will try to demonstrate my intentions in my
(now following) absolutely own part, and
conclusion, of this letter.

There are, in the actual work of drawing
a design for a type face, three stages. This
our craft has in common with many an
other craft and with several arts. The first
stage, being nearest the conception and in
fact part and parcel of the conception itself,
is the best. — Here our craft differs from
music: what the composer hears, before
he has written one single note on his paper,
is the music; and so the conception, going
before the notation, is completely interior.
There is, however, in this respect a great
similarity of type design and sculpture:
as long as what the sculptor sees with his
mind's eye has not gotten form in some
matter, that is equally rebellious as I
have said the familiar letter forms to be,
there is nothing. I have intentionally
chosen this example in order to be able to

29

point out the incredible greatness of
Michelangelo's prisoners and Pieta in the
Accademia in Florence as compared with
his other sculptures in the Nuova Sagrestia
of San Lorenzo, in the same city, his David,
also in the Accademia, or his Moses and
Pieta in Rome. Whether you deem the prisoners and first mentioned Pieta to be completed or not I think you shall have to admit
that their greater greatness is due to their
being so much nearer the conceptional stage
than the other, polished, masterworks I have
also mentioned. (With all this I will of
course not say that the difference of class
between sculpture and type design is not
maintained never to be forgotten.)—For
those people possibly reading this essay who
are less familiar with the works of Michelangelo I have dealt with than you and I are

30

I am adding photographs of the Madonna col Figlio, in the Nuova Sagrestia, and of the Pietà di Palestrina, in the Accademia (Centro Michelangiolesco), both at Firenze.

The first stage of a drawing for type design will as a rule be in a material, say pencil, that is erasable and, so, easily corrected; it will not be too precise or exact: the intention of the designer is just somewhere in his vague lines. The next, or middle, stage will be in pencil lines that leave little to guess. And the final one, as neat as the designer is able to execute it, in carbon ink; that is if he is not presumptuous enough to think that he can judge his own work without seeing it as near as possible what it is meant for: in full black on white.— It is remarkable that the general practice with draughtsmen working for mechanical cutting of punches is that no filled-in drawings are made and that, as a rule, their drawings are reversed at that!

I am sending you, with this letter, a drawing — it is by no means a design since it is not meant as such — which I have made as long before there ever had been question of my writing the letter as after my latest, maybe my last, design for a type face. I have, honestly, not tried to prove my point in making this drawing; I have, on the contrary, endeavoured not to prove it, by maintaining the qualities of the first stage through the second and third stages, but I have not succeeded; & my point has proved itself. As you will see I have started drawing the same few characters three times all over. I have left the first row in pencil where I think

32

the mise au point, also in pencil, should normally begin; the second row I have carried through this mise au point; the third row I have completed by filling it in.

In looking at the drawing, and I have looked at it quite a number of times, I have always found, as I still find, that the first row is the most interesting one and therefore the best; it certainly is the best representation of my intentions vague though they may show. The next row is still tolerable; while the last, the filled-in one, has, to my taste, lost most of its interest. — This, by the way, more or less proves that one is wrong in reproaching the pantograph punch-cutting machine, as John Lewis and John Brinkley do, of producing a dehumanized version of what may have been a sprightly original. Does not the dehumanization start already

33

under the hands of the designer? And if
it does not, for instance with designers who
are at the same time better draughtsmen than
I am — and, if not most, at least many of
them are —, is it not then likely to lose its
sprightliness in the drawing office where
the working drawings, for the patterns to
be worked from in the punch-cutting machine,
are made?

I think after all that it might be best,
when the co-operation between designer and
punch-cutter is sufficiently close, to have the
punch-cutter work after drawings in their
first stage; in them there is a maximum of
sprightliness and the team of two will have
little trouble in making the necessary corrections where the intentions of the designer might have been insufficiently clear
or distinct in his drawing.

34

From the first I am coming to the third, the filled in, drawing which, I think, has to be made at any event; as I have said before: how could the designer judge of what is going to happen without it? It can be photographed down to several actual body sizes; it can be worked on, if necessary, to make corrections; in short it really is indispensable. But as it has lost so much already since the first stage of the design it had better not be used for any practical working purpose.

Having dealt with the beginning and the end of the drawings and, I hope, explained what is good or bad in them I may venture to say that in the cutting of punches by hand there are no problems like those as are haunting me. — A good designer who is an able punch-cutter himself will make good, maybe the best possible, work; a good designer &

a good punch-cutter, collaborating with him, will perhaps produce equally good things; losses in quality, on either side, will have the consequences one may expect; and they will be reflected in the couple's performances. But all of these people's achievements will be characteristically the work of human hands which although it may have its disadvantages will show the charms of such work.)

I am afraid, as I told you, that it is not far from being a dying craft. And there is, therefore, the more reason to reflect upon what can be done to improve the products of the punch-cutting machine which, according to Updike — and he is neither too apodictical nor, as certain other people are, devoid of hope—, "tends to mechanize the design of types". — It is put a bit strangely when seen from a certain angle but it is a

36

wise observation fundamentally.— What would one expect: the punch-cutting machine is a mechanism; how, then, could it be otherwise than that this mechanism tends to mechanize the product that was before made by hand? But what Updike really, and wisely, says is that the machine has a mechanizing influence on the design itself; whether he means this or not I am unable to say. And, if he does mean it, it is quite possible that what he has detected is not a fault in the punch-cutting machine but a shortcoming of the drawing office that could, though not easily, be corrected. This, however, is a point I can not expatiate on now since it would lead me too far afield.

From my so far not having discussed the second drawing — or, normally, the

drawing's second stage — you will already
have understood that it is the one I should like
to intend as a model for the drawing office
that precedes the actual punch-cutting: a
model for the working drawing after which
the pattern for the machine is made.

In order to make its use for this purpose
possible it has to be painstakingly exact
and precise and as free as any man's hand
is able to make it from characteristics that
betray that very hand. — It is for this reason,
and not for this reason only, that a so-called
copy of an existing type face to be made by
machine is an anomaly. It has, in its characteristic lines, to be slavishly followed in the
working drawing; and the slightest irregularities, left in it by the designer's hand,
have to be done away with.

This procedure, and this only, would

yield the true machine made type. Whether it would be satisfactory remains, surprising as it may seem, to be seen; since for aught I know there has so far never been made type strictly according to these rules. I see no reason why, when it would be criticized, sprightly and inhuman should be opposed to each other: it could be sprightly even if dehumanized. But in its austerely mechanical appearance it would have won the human virtue of honesty. And you may know that, here too, it is honesty I am after.

Ever yours sincerely

Jan van Krimpen

MICHELANGELO ⁄ LA PIETÀ DI PALESTRINA
Centro Michelangelo ⁄ Florence

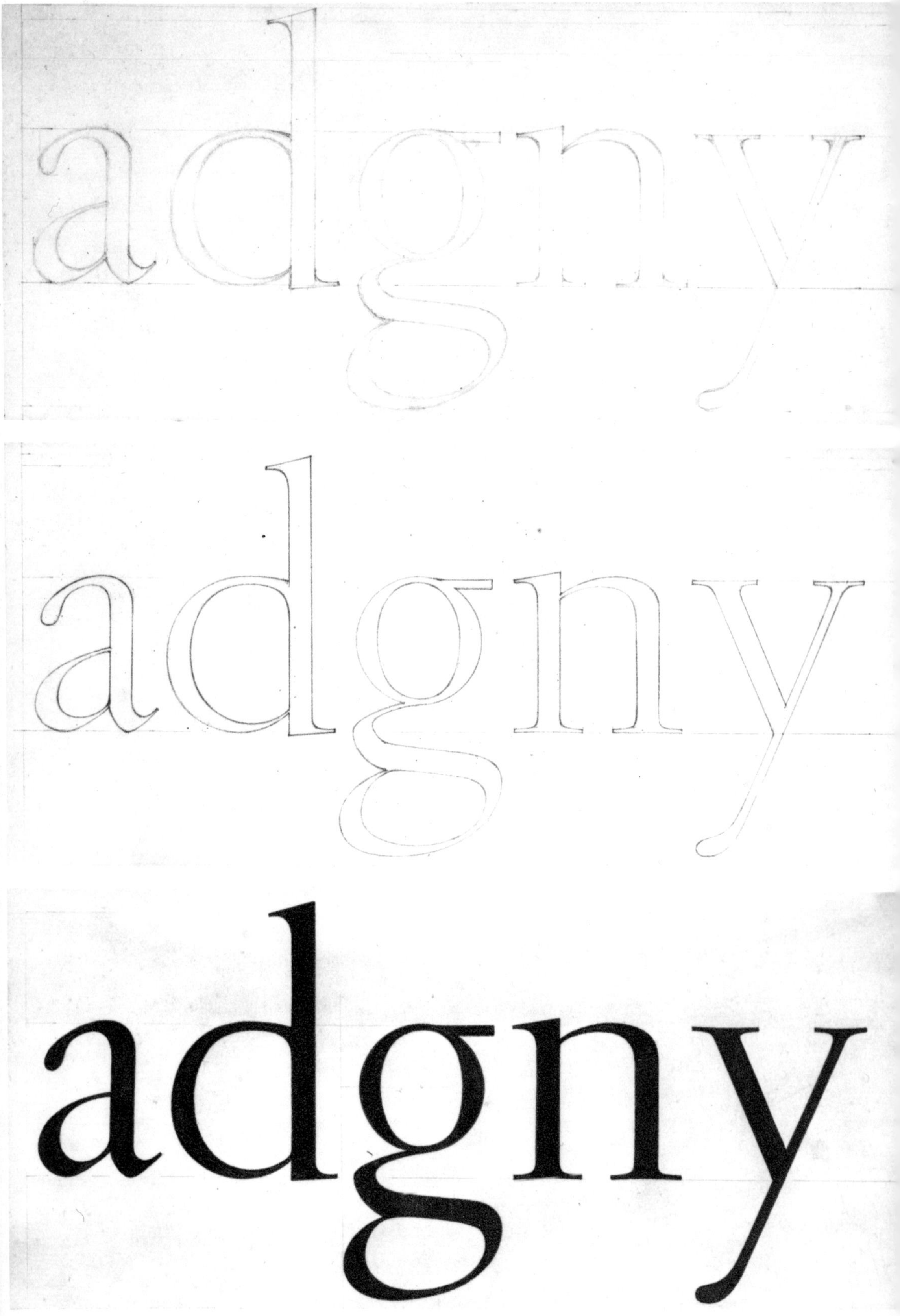
adgny
adgny
adgny

APPENDIXES

APPENDIX 1
SELECT HANDLIST OF TYPOGRAPHICAL
WRITINGS BY JAN VAN KRIMPEN

1. 'Typography in Holland' in *The Fleuron*, no. VII (Cambridge, University Press and Doubleday Doran & Co., 1930), pp. 1–24.

2. *Het Huis Enschedé 1703–1953* (Haarlem, Enschedé en Zonen, 1953) contains 'Een korte Geschiedenis van het bedrijf door J. van Krimpen'.

3. A paragraph of some 120 words expressing Van Krimpen's views on book illustration was quoted by Hellmut Lehmann-Haupt on p. 18 of his introductory notes to the catalogue *International Book Illustration 1935–1945*, an exhibition sponsored by the American Institute of Graphic Arts and held from September to October, 1946 at the Pierpont Morgan Library, New York.

4. 'Plantin and Our Time'. A paper delivered at the Plantin celebrations in Antwerp, 1955, and subsequently published in *Gedenkboek der Plantin-Dagen. 1555–1955* (Antwerp, 1956), pp. 250–9.

5. 'A letter to Philip Hofer on certain problems connected with the mechanical cutting of punches'. Heemstede, November, 1955. Reproduced in facsimile and discussed at length in this book.

6. 'A Perspective on Design'. An address delivered to the Society of Industrial Artists in London on 17 December 1956, after Van Krimpen received the Society's Design Award; subsequently printed in the *Journal of the Society of Industrial Artists* (London, February 1957), pp. 24–7, and in *Printing and Graphic Arts*, vol. 5 (Lunenburg, Vermont, 1957), pp. 1–4.

7. An essay of some 1300 words with no title was contributed by Van Krimpen to a pamphlet, *Inspired Typography 1966*, circulated by

The Type Directors Club of New York in connection with a forum held on 3 April 1956 at which the subject of the pamphlet was discussed. Van Krimpen disregarded the date in the title, but gave a characteristic statement of his attitude to the practice of typography.

8. *On Designing and Devising Type* (1957). pp. [1]–109. This book was issued as their 32nd Chap Book by The Typophiles of New York, but extra copies were printed with special imprints for Joh. Enschedé en Zonen, Haarlem; H.D. Tjeenk Willink & Zoon, Haarlem; The Sylvan Press, London; A.A. Balkema, Capetown; Paul Jammes, Paris; and 'Heemstede: The Author'.

9. 'On Related Type Faces' in *Book Design and Production*, vol. 1 (London, 1958), pp. 28–30.

10. 'First Steps Toward the Roman Letter' in *Printing and Graphic Arts* (Lunenburg, Vermont, 1959), vol. 7, pp. 20–3. A note by the editor explains that this essay was 'intended as an introduction to a projected book on constructed roman letters, which has only progressed so far at the time of the author's sudden illness and death'.

11. 'A Perspective on Type and Typography' in *Printing and Graphic Arts* (Lunenburg, Vermont, 1959), vol. 7, pp. 93–109. Van Krimpen sent a note on this text to Professor Ray Nash on 3 October, 1958, in which he wrote '…by the way, as soon as I got back from France, early in August, I put pen to paper to write down my "formal" lecture to be delivered whenever it should be wanted. It is, practically speaking, ready by now. If I should still come it would serve its intended purpose; if not you may have it to do with it what you like. It is essentially a lecture, though, and not an essay and I cannot think of rewriting it, with additions and deletions, so as to make it a real essay'. The manuscript was sent to Professor Nash by the author's widow on 9 February 1959, and was then sub-edited before publication.

APPENDIX 2
LETTER FROM STANLEY MORISON TO
JAN VAN KRIMPEN, 5 MARCH 1956

Parts of this letter were quoted by Van Krimpen in his Typophile Chap Book (1957) but he inverted the third point in Morison's penultimate paragraph, thereby seriously misrepresenting the original.

43 Fetter Lane, London, E.C.4., 5th March 1956

Dear van Krimpen,

Many thanks for the memorandum. I am not so sure that, properly understood, my standpoint differs to a radical extent from your own.

I have not *The Tally* at hand, and do not remember what is in it. I may well have failed to explain myself, because the whole thing was written at great speed, at Crutchley's request, and I felt at the time that the kind of book it was going to be had better not be published. However, I doubt if I said, or intended to say, that I was pleased as Pierpont* with the Poliphilo.

It is necessary to be very careful, writing and considering these matters we now are, not to read into 1922 what we think after the experience of 30 years or more. I think I told you once, that I might one day put pen to paper on this 30 years' experience for the purpose of denying as well as affirming or re-affirming positions I had taken up at certain times. This is a factor you

---

* F.H.Pierpont was described by Morison in *A Tally of Types* as the head of the Monotype works. Morison found him to be a forceful character who strongly opposed 'interference from the head office' and who was 'a notorious upholder of the sovereignty of staff engineers, of practical accomplishments and of accepted values'.

leave out of account in your memorandum, which might be worth discussing.

It may be that this is the real point at which you and I divide. When I, for better or worse, became interested in what is now called typography, the prevailing doctrine was firmly set, not by the typographers (for the simple reason that there were none) but by the calligraphers (of whom there were many), and these calligraphers were learned as well as expert. They dominated the situation in this country and, to a considerable extent in Germany, upon which country Britain depended for a good deal of its 'display' material. It was a world dominated by Johnston, Graily Hewitt, Percy Smith on the one hand, and St. John Hornby and the private presses on the other.

It is possible that where you and I differ, is in the relative assessment we give to the crafts of calligraphy and engraving. I have been at great pains to maintain the engraving craft in the service of typography; to graft from the old tree of the hand-engraver upon the young sapling of the machine punchcutter. This, you will say, is the wrong way to graft. If the hand punch-cutters had been numerous enough to organize themselves so as to take command of the machine I doubt very much whether you or I would have much to debate; the difficulty would have been solved, and engravers would have used the machine in accordance with their own traditional capacity. As it was, the machine fell into the hands of engineers who knew nothing about letter design fifty years ago – and know nothing to this day.

The various expedients resorted to by me to get a punch-cutter from Frankfurt and so forth were unavailing.

My next effort was to seize upon Gill's Perpetua as a sculptured script. How far successful it is in type is not for us to say. At least it corresponded with my intentions. The Times type is an attempt to draw upon Bristol board an engraved-looking letter. It was, however, never engraved, – as in the case of Perpetua. Hence, The Times type only [partially] realises my intentions.

There are many things in your memorandum worth pondering; but I think you need not have brought such heavy guns to bear upon mock antique. I see nothing of the mock antique in our Bembo, or in Mardersteig's.

There are other points, however, on which I think you rather overstate our differences. I do not really believe that you mean that Monotype and foundry type are two essentially different things. I do not believe these differences are essential. I believe they are different but I question whether the difference is so great. However, this is merely a matter of verbal expression.

I am certainly all for your appreciation of the 'designer' and his 'intentions' – when he knows himself what he 'wants'. You appreciate quite rightly the importance of a 'designer' who understands his job. I am not sure, though, that this is the same thing as a designer who understands what the job is. I am all for the doctrine that 'the soul, so to say, of any design lies in its subtleties'. Certainly neither I nor anybody else attached to this Institution, wishes, or ever has wished, to eliminate hand punch-cutting. That elimination has been achieved by the typefounders.

In saying what you do say in behalf of the hand-cut punches, you have to wrestle with the problem created by the fact that the hand-cutting of punches is a defunct art. You may have one, and Peignot may have one, but these men are, in point of actual fact, without apprentices. I would lament this quite as fully as you do. I would agree that the 'best hand-cut punches are superior to any machine-cut ones'.

I hold, however, that, in the last thirty years or so, due to the calligraphical doctrine I mentioned earlier, typography has been made to bear the weight of all sorts of calligraphical experiments, many of which went far to break down the true (as I hold them to be) standards of type-cutting. Thus came in a flood of pseudo-calligraphic designs. These are fully as open to the philosophical objections that you bring against Poliphilo.

Indeed, I am not sure whether your own solution to our difficulty is not itself open to philosophical objections. You limit the Works to the right of smoothing out imperfections and irregularities of design made by a man who understands his job.

I do not see in your letter any definition, still less description, of that 'job'. I suspect, however, that such a designer, if not warned against it, will be under the impression that he is designing a 'type' – whereas what he is doing is making a design. He has got his units right, he has done all the necessary preliminary work to the mechanical engraving of a design. This design he has produced on Bristol board or squared paper or whatever it is he chooses. Thus finished, he brings it to the Works, in accordance with your requirement that the best result can only be obtained by having a design originally made for the Monotype. As you say 'originally made'. The Works then, and in accordance with the right you concede, perform their task of making any smoothing out that may be in their opinion desirable, and in the designer's tolerable. This is where the designer leaves it.

I am prepared to say, at this point, 'so far so good'. I have not it here, but I have a vague recollection of a polemical piece written against Graily Hewitt.* I would not be surprised if there is something in it which is relevant to the matter before us.

Do you, or do you not stand with me in recognizing the fact

that roman type from the end of the fifteenth century down to the twentieth century, was a casting from a mould made for the purpose of embodying a matrix struck from a hand-engraved punch? Secondly, do you stand with me in believing that four hundred years of such engraving creates in the image printed from these castings a second nature which is so strong as to be unchangeable? Thirdly, do you stand with me in believing that the imitation of the work of the hand-engraver by the hand-calligrapher is open to the same objection that you bring to Pierpont's pathetic self-satisfaction with his imitation of Poliphilo – with all warts? If you and I agree upon these three points, then we can agree upon everything.

I dictate this clean off the belly, on a fine, sunny morning. Pay no more attention to it than it deserves....

Yours, STANLEY MORISON

* The reference is to an unsigned review by Morison of 'The Treyford Type, designed by Graily Hewitt exclusively for the University Press, Oxford, 1929. (14 point size.)' in *The Fleuron*, no. VII (Cambridge 1930), pp. 180–185. The following three extracts are particularly relevant:

'It seems to be necessary to insist that type is an engraved not a written thing, and that the punch-cutter's position in typefounding has not been completely superseded by the modern engraving machines. For several reasons, not we think always borne in mind by Mr Hewitt, it is the punch-cutter's craft which changes script into type. The punch-cutter can indeed, by engraving a facsimile of the calligraphic model, produce a printing letter like the Treyford, but this would be rather a *tour de force* than a normal use of his skill.'

'The transition from old-face to modern was not so much a matter of typographical design as of punch-cutting technique; to wit, the relation between thick and thin, and serif construction. These refinements have little or no connection with calligraphy.'

'The engraver's accomplished hand and logical mind, freed from calligraphical prejudice, enabled him to succeed directly where no scribe dare hope for more than a compromise: he formalised his lower-case and assimilated it to the upper-case taken over from the classical inscriptions by unifying the serif treatment. Thus he gave serifed feet to m n p l f h etc. Mr Hewitt therefore is not, in our opinion, welcome to dismiss the printer as a mere corrupt imitator of the more highly endowed scribe.'

This book has been printed in an edition of 2000
copies by Joh. Enschedé en Zonen, Haarlem,
and bound by Jansen, Leiden.
The type is Spectrum, the last of the three
'Monotype' faces designed by Jan van Krimpen.
The paper was specially made for this book
by Schut, Heelsum, The Netherlands.
S. L. Hartz and Bram de Does were
responsible for the design.

This book is a joint publication of
The Harvard College Library
&
David R. Godine.